How to Manage a Behavior Classroom

The Beginner's Guide to Teaching the Emotionally Disabled
and the Oppositional Defiant Child

By: Don and Kellie Rainwater

Why I Wrote This Book

Some people ask me why I wrote this book. Although I am not an expert on behavior and I have completed one behavior class in my master's program in college, and I have also worked with emotionally disabled and oppositional defiant children for the last six years. Though most mainstream teachers and even some special education teachers shun the behavior classroom, I found that the behavior classroom is the best place to connect with children and help them through difficult times of stress and frustration.

The behavior classroom is a classroom like none other on earth. One deals more with behaviors and how to modify behaviors than they deal with the basics, such as reading, writing, and arithmetic. An entire day may be spent dealing with one student, but at the end of the day results are recognized. These children have a need to know that they are loved and have a safe place to be. Public schools can be a very unsettling and intimidating experience for most students with emotional disabilities. These students might feel alone in a sea of faces and it may be overwhelming for some of these young children.

When you become a teacher of a behavior classroom, you may be just as misunderstood as the children that you teach. Behavior classes become a dumping ground not only for mainstream teachers but also for special educators and administrative faculty. These children are the kids that are rejected in their classrooms so there is a need to take the children and show them that you love them and that they can improve their behavior.

Though there are a few articles on the Internet about behavior classrooms, when I was looking for ideas for my own classroom, I could not find completed research. The ideas and principles within this book use simple language and derive themselves solely from experience and there is no research-based knowledge included. Some people refer to the behavior teacher just a warm body to take care of the unruly and unmanageable. There is no formal training and you, as the teacher, have to improvise most the time. Anybody with a special education degree can teach behavior children, but it takes a consistently patient and understanding teacher to deal with the stress and trauma of the classroom daily.

As you read through these pages, remember these processes are not written in stone. Each classroom and student deals with a behavior program as an individual and needs to be treated as an individual. These are only fundamental guidelines to help the beginning behavior teacher have an understanding on what they should know and some of the problems and types of students they might have in their classroom. So take these recommendations and ideas and make them your own but add to it your own personality, your own sense of value and morals, and add in a big heart with a compassionate view of the world and you will forever impact the lives of the students that you teach in behavior programs.

The Behavior Classroom: Program and Teacher

Most public schools have a behavior program included either in the special education program or through affiliated programs outside the school. The behavior program or a special education program is specifically designed to deal with kids who have emotional disabilities or Oppositional Defiance Disorder. Each child is placed into a program where they are self-contained and then they can slowly work their way into the mainstream population. If you are put into a classroom that services behavior children, you need to know the nuances of how to create an environment in which they can learn, not only the core subjects of education, but also how to behave well in society.

This book will explain to you how to set up your behavior classroom to not only exemplify the education, but also to maintain an atmosphere of discipline and work ethic. You must be able to learn about the specific student you will encounter and also the referral process which they will go through to get into your program. The basis of this book is from behavior programs in eastern Wyoming. Your state may have different programs that are similar but with different ideals.

A good behavior specialist needs a degree in special education and some experience in dealing with emotional disabilities. Sometimes, special education teachers that work in the lower IQ classrooms, and deal with these students regularly, are a great candidate for the position. It takes a lot of patience to work with these students. The person chosen for the position must be able to keep calm in very adverse situations and model appropriate behavior at all times. Regardless of whether it is a perceived or real crisis, your students will react in a way that you have never experienced before in other classrooms.

The behavior classroom teacher also needs to have the foreknowledge that he/she is not like the other teachers. You need to concentrate on the behavior of the child first and then the education second. If the child cannot maintain themselves to stay focused or to pay attention long enough to do an assignment, then they will never be able to join the mainstream by graduating from the program. You must be concerned that the child may have no social skills, little self-esteem, acting out behaviors, or oppositional defiance.

A teacher hired for this job should have a heart filled with compassion and exhibit the patience of Job. The burnout rate for behavior teachers is approximately two years. Most people only last a year in a program before they try to look for other work. It takes a very special person to stay in the field and to make the study and applications of behavior modeling a way of life. You will find that by helping these children through life, you will receive more of a reward than an ordinary paycheck. You will touch the lives of children who most people want to avoid. The following text explains in detail how to work with each child and how to set up your classroom and instruction to bring some enlightenment to otherwise lost children.

The Behavior Child

When you first begin to teach a behavior classroom, you may not have experience dealing with all the problems of the children that you might run into. Some of the kids have severe attention deficits and hyperactivity. They cannot sit still for a second without being distracted. Most of these children are on medication, but sometimes the lack of supervision at home does not allow them to take their medication on a consistent basis. Other children may not take medication at all, due to the parents' belief that their children should not be medicated. The ADHD child in the behavior room has to learn how to stay on task and also how not to let distractions bother them.

Of these students, one out of two children will be emotionally disturbed. This could range from mild to severe. Those children with severe behavior problems could be one step away from a placement in your room. The severe behavior child will have acting out behavior and will not be able to socialize within the classroom in an acceptable manner. Often, it emerges that a disabled child has severe anxiety over social situations. These behaviors will affect their academic performance and how they solve problems.

The children that come into your classroom are usually the children that the mainstream teachers cannot handle and even the administration has almost given up on. While in the mainstream, they may have gotten multiple write-ups or been sent to the office for disciplinary problems. Oftentimes the behavior classroom becomes a dumping ground for all the behaviors of the school. If you plan to lead a successful behavior program, you will need to set guidelines about who comes into your class and how long they will remain.

You should have a structured program, that will be discussed later, which will have an entrance and exit strategy for the student. Unfortunately, when the administration sees that you are having success with students, they will give you more students to take the brunt of the labor from other classroom teachers. Sometimes this situation becomes a political nightmare in which other teachers and administration will use your classroom instead of trying to correct the behaviors themselves.

The students you will receive are mainly damaged from family situations, such as severe abuse or neglect. When you work with them in your room, you should consider the possibility that the emotional disturbance could be stemming from the home environment. Ideally, they should have a nurturing family and environment at home despite having disabilities so severe that they cannot control their own behavior. These children are often withdrawn or have angry outbursts, which not only causes stress to the student, but also the staff and the rest of the class. This kind of student is the most challenging of all. They will probably stay in the behavior program until they graduate or end up in a facility or a correctional institution.

How to Set Up Your Behavior Classroom

Before the school year starts, you usually have a week or so to get your classroom prepared. The behavior classroom needs to be set up differently than other classrooms. You will not be lecturing or standing at a podium in this classroom, but you will be on your feet, making sure your children are on task and behaving appropriately.

The first issue is desks. Traditional desks typically do not work well in the behavior classroom. The best desks are usually self-contained with blinders on either side and a blinder in front. This way, the child has their own space where they cannot see from side to side or forward unless they twist their body around in the chair. This will allow the children little distraction by movements or anything else that might be happening in the room.

The desk should also be big enough to be used as a personal space. The students can decorate the inside of the blinders with pictures or cutouts so that the seating can be individualized and make them feel like it is their own safe place. Most behavior children do not use lockers, so they keep most of their belongings at their desk or in the desk area. Provide a coat rack for coats and backpacks and drawers for their personal items that they do not want others to have.

The desks should be facing away from the teacher's desk. This way you can see what is going on without walking around the room. They should be angled away from each other so one child cannot turn around and directly interact with another child. This may take some creativity, and the room may not have an organized look, but if you put a behavior child next to another, trouble is sure to erupt. Sometimes a semicircle or small cluster is best. Another strategy includes putting the desk against the wall and angling it away from other desks so the child cannot interact.

You should also have a couple of worktables in the room. These tables and chairs should be of heavy construction. Behavior children like to throw desks and chairs when throwing temper tantrums and they seem to enjoy watching them fly through the air like a missile. Use the worktables for group work or in a one-on-one setting. Make sure the surface of the table is washable, because behavior children like to deface desks and chairs with crayons, pencils, or anything they can get their hands on.

Your desk should be clear of anything that could be used as missiles, also. This includes scissors, staplers, heavy books, coffee cups, or anything else that can be thrown at another child. Behavior children are often thieves and will take whatever they want. So make sure that your personal belongings, such as purse, keys, or even family pictures, are safely secured. Some of these children will take your personal belongings just to get back at you because you disciplined them.

How to Decorate Your Behavior Classroom

Now that you have your desks and tables arranged in your classroom, you must think about what to put on the walls. Most classrooms have a wide variety of posters and educational materials, but you may want to tone down the decorations. For the ADHD child or any child who has concentration problems, a room with bright colors and posters with a lot of pictures can drive their mind into a world of fantasy.

The behavior classroom should have as little on the walls as possible. You should have your rules and your expectations for behavior posted on the wall. Simple colored sheets that explain how to ask for directions, how to enter a conversation, how to ask for help, and other social situations are the best. That way if the child is looking up and looking around the room, the only thing they will see is the directions to put them back on task. You also do not wish to have anything that has a lot of numbers or letters on it. This is very confusing for the ADHD child and they will read the same message over and over if you let them.

During the holidays, you will want to keep the decorations to a minimum. The children can get overly excited when it's close to Winter Break. Anything that reminds them of school being let out for the next two or three days can push them into frenzy. Any item such as a Christmas tree, with all the color and shining objects, distracts a child and has them daydreaming about Christmas morning. Any holiday can be a distraction and it is not wise to have a countdown to the holiday. Some teachers write on their blackboard how many days are left at school or how many days until the school break. This can cause a lot of distraction in the behavior classroom that will be too much for some children to bear.

The best decorations for a behavior classroom are plants. Plants, which are green and leafy, give a calming effect to the room. Of course you will have the prankster who will try to kill the plant by pouring something into the soil, but if you place some hanging plants out of reach, the calming effect of the green color will give life to your room and at the same time, calm your children. The timeout room should have no decorations in it whatsoever.

The decoration of your room is, of course, your choice. However, you will need to think ahead and determine what each potential item to be placed on the wall will or will not do for a child that is behaviorally challenged. A little forethought will save you months of grief and keep you from having to tear down something that you paid a lot of money for, or put a great deal of time or effort into.

The Timeout Room

When you plan how you will design your classroom for a behavior student body, the timeout room is an important consideration. Most timeout rooms consist of a room about the size of a large closet with no furniture. It should have a heavy institutional door that will stand up to kids banging and kicking against it. There should be no locks on the timeout room door. If a child is in a timeout room and tries to escape they are breaking the rules of the program and must deal with the consequences. Only in extreme measures, which are approved by the parent, the administration, and the school, should a child be locked inside a timeout room. You should also review your state's laws to find out if locking the door is a fire hazard or opposes child abuse laws.

The timeout room should have a window that you can look through to make sure the child is not harming themselves. The window should be reinforced so that the child cannot bang their head or smash their fist into it and end up hurting or cutting themselves in some way. The timeout room should have the fixtures high above the child's reach where they cannot get hold of a light bulb or florescent tubing and cut themselves with the glass. There should be no plugs or electrical outlets inside the timeout room that the child might stick their finger into or otherwise try to harm themselves. The child should have nothing in their pockets when going to the timeout room. This includes pencils or anything that can cause harm. Many behavior children and emotionally disabled children will hurt themselves when they are in an emotional crisis.

When you use the timeout room, you need to watch the child's behavior. Most timeout rooms have both drywall or cinder block walls and many behavior children will bang their heads or punch the walls. When a child is exhibiting this type of behavior, you need to walk in and tell them to stop. If they will not stop hurting themselves, then you need to contact the administration and the parents immediately. Shout down the hall for a helper or paraprofessional. Do not touch the child, but keep them from hurting themselves when they are attempting to slam their head against the wall. Place your body so that you become a human shield that will absorb the blows that the child is aiming at the wall. At the point where they are slamming their head against you or punching you, the child has become assaultive and it is out of the hands of the school's administration. Basically, when they hit you or cause you pain because of their actions, they are beyond the limitations of your program and special education.

Make sure you understand the timeout room laws and child restraint laws in your district and state before you ever place a child into timeout. Make sure that the parents understand the procedures of timeout. After agreeing to the procedures, the parents should sign a document stating that they understand what timeout is and that the child will be placed in the room without furniture and without contact. But also reassure the parents that their child will be under observation at all times when they are in the timeout space. It is best to keep a list of contact information of the students' parents, the administration, and immediate help from nearby for you to be able to call during an emergency situation. You might even want to have the parents on speed dial so that you don't make a mistake while dialing in a hurry.

Even though your school may have a policy against cell phone use, talk to your administration about being allowed to carry one. There is no place so sacred that you will not have a behavior problem, whether it is in the hallways or walking back from the gym. Sometimes, in your behavior teaching career you will have a child completely lose control and you need immediate help. Have the necessary people on speed dial in your cell phone and contact them when you see a situation getting out of hand.

The Teacher's Desk

A teacher's desk is not only the sanctity of the teacher's private things, but also the centerpiece of the room. If you have a room that is void of space and storage areas, why not open up your desk to everyone in the room. Most desks have a lot of drawers in which you can put your purse, wallet, or other private things that you do not want touched. The best desk has plenty of room for all the materials that a student or aide might need. The center drawer can be used for pencils, paper clips, and the basic stationery items used that day. The side doors can be used to store files, books, crayons, or teaching materials that you might need. If you keep it organized and available to everybody in the class, the teacher's desk will become a storage unit for the classroom.

The surface of the teacher's desk should be clean, except for what is being worked on at the moment, and the workspace should be able to hold a few personal items such as family pictures, or other items that might exemplify the personality of the teacher. The desk should be set in the center of the room so that all students can easily access it without being out of sight or supervision of the teacher. Don't place any money, cell phones, or any item that students can steal. Cell phones are a big temptation, especially in middle school. Sometimes it is best to place them on a shelf or storage in the teacher's desk. This way the teacher will have better organization and be able to direct the students quickly to the item that is needed.

If a teacher spends a few days at the beginning of the year training students where to get supplies, how to handle those supplies in a responsible way, and how to replace them properly, it will save valuable time obtaining a pencil or eraser for a student. Also the teacher should train the aide or paraprofessional that is in the room to reinforce the training they are giving students and so they are able to go into the desk without a problem. Some people think a person's desk is their private area. You need to consider that your students will have more access to the materials they need, if they have access to your desk and you will have more storage space in your classroom.

Before The First Day of School

The first day of school in a behavior classroom can be very unsettling. It is a time for you, as a teacher, to set the standards for the year. A good rule of thumb is to visit the children you know will be in your room, the spring before the new school year starts. This way, they will come into your room without having the anxiety of not being familiar with you. Talk with their former teacher and find out what behaviors they displayed, what progress was made and any other information, academically or behaviorally, that you should know.

Review their IEP files and read about the documented behavior in the past and how much growth they have made. The IEP should give you a roadmap to where the child began and where he is now. You should also be aware of summer regression. Sometimes the child forgets everything they were taught the year before during the summer break. You should, therefore, make a formal assessment to reassess the child's skills after he first returns to school. This regression can happen both academically and behaviorally, so be prepared. The child that you read about in the IEP may not be the same child on the first day of school.

Have your behavior plan all laid out so that you and your paraprofessional know exactly what to do and say whenever any situation arises. A good behavior plan is something that you can create yourself. You can perform research on the Internet, to find more information about successful strategies that have worked for others. You may be able to talk to a behavior teacher before the children come to your class, so you know what kind of rules and guidelines they had, and perhaps follow the same setup. The Boy's Town Model is a good model to follow. Even if you decide not to follow the model precisely, you can take some good information from it.

Have all your supplies and materials ready to go on the first day of school. It is good to have a full cup of sharpened pencils, crayons, glue, and all of the things the child will need for the rest of the year, set out and ready to give to them. Most behavior children are unorganized and it is a good idea to have three-ring binders with all of their class information placed in them. Each child should have a spiral notebook from which they can pull out paper as needed. Loose-leaf paper is often a nuisance and becomes soiled or wrinkled before it can be used.

Have the students' names on the desks and chairs so they know where to go when they arrive on the first day of school. Stand beside the front door and greet each child as they come through the door. Look them directly in the eye, acknowledge them, and give some pleasantry. How you treat the student when he first enters the door will be how the student treats you for the rest of the year. Always give eye-contact and smile. If you see the student acting out as soon as he gets to the classrooms, quietly walk over to him/her and ask them to take a seat. Many students are nervous about meeting a new teacher, so most often the student will comply.

On the First Day of School

The bell rang and the first day of school began. You will probably have anywhere from four to eight students in a behavior classroom. You should bring them all together in a circle. Have them sit on the ground and be quiet. Explain the rules to them slowly and maybe even role-play a few of the behaviors you want them to display. Explain to them what redirection is and how to accept it. Also, explain the rewards and consequences in your classroom.

Schedules are very important and whether they're young or in high school, a student wants to know where and when they're supposed to do something. After explaining the rules, consequences, rewards, and behavior models, you should go over how the students will be expected to behave. This is a time to explain that as soon as they walk through your door, they are to follow your class rules. They are to put away their jackets and their book bags and get prepared for the day of learning. Also, explain that once the bell rings, they need to be sitting quietly, awaiting instructions.

The first day will be a little hectic. A lot of confusion will surface once the kids try to test you, both with their behavior and their inability to follow directions. The first student that is redirected and ends up in a timeout will set the standard of understanding that you are the one setting the rules and you will enforce them.

The first day of school should be dedicated to setting rules and schedules. Do not perform any assessment during this time. You might want to try a few fun things to see where your students are. Play a board game or break out the puzzles and let them have an easy day. This way, you can see which children will work well together and who has a competitive spirit that will end up disrupting the class or committing an outburst.

The first day of school, you should focus on getting to know your students. Let them know that you're the person they should come to with any problems. You are the one who will listen to them and guide them through the next school year. You expect respect from your students and they should know that respect is not freely given. Just as they are expected to earn respect, you must earn theirs as well. Never make promises that you cannot keep and never go back on your word.

Set the tone the first day, but refrain from being too strict. Stick to your rules and work through levels of behavior that you expect the child to follow, without being overbearing. Confront the very important issues but you should let the lesser important issues slide until the next day. Teach various lessons about behavior as you go through the day. Make sure students understand what they're expected to do and what the consequences will be if they do not follow the set rules. Remember, they are behavior children and they will try to test you.

The Behavior Plan

Developing a behavior plan should not be too difficult. First you have to look at what behavior you want corrected, and then you decide how you want to correct it. For example, if you have a rule against talking without raising your hand, then you should have a plan to realign inappropriate behavior. A simple basic plan can be to start with only a redirection. A redirection is what happens when you tell a student not to behave a certain way.

For example, a boy speaks out without raising his hand. You should look at that student, directly in the eye, and without raising your voice, say, "You need to raise your hand before you speak." If the child does not change the behavior, then you will need to redirect. You do this by saying, "This is your first redirection. You need to raise your hand before you speak or you will be given a second redirection or may choose to take a voluntary timeout." At this point the student decides whether they will follow the directions and behave or if they will take a time out for five minutes. If the student decides to take the time out, then you let them take the timeout and discuss the situation with them later. If the child does not change his behavior immediately, you need to give a second redirection.

The second redirection needs to be spoken calmly again, "You need to raise your hand before you speak. This is your second redirection. If you do not change your behavior, you will have a mandatory timeout." If the child does not change their behavior, they should be put into the timeout room. If you are with the child in a mainstream classroom when this occurs, the child should be asked to leave the room. Then they should be escorted back to the behavior room where they will be put into a timeout. Place the child in the timeout room for a minimum of five minutes. You may see some bizarre behaviors. The children may talk to themselves, beat or kick the walls, or scream.

Once the child has de-escalated and/or their time has ended, walk into the timeout room and ask them if they are ready to progress. If they choose to progress, then the child can discuss the occurrence with you. If the child does not want to progress, close the door and give them five more minutes. Another chapter will discuss how to deal with the child in the timeout room.

If the child becomes violent and looks like he is a danger to himself or others, contact administration and the parents. Let the parents know that they should pick up the child. Document all violent outbursts. If you choose to use a video camera in your room, you must get parental permission to videotape the students before the school year begins. This is a basic behavior plan on how to handle individual behavior. The next chapter will discuss the levels of behavior and how to give rewards and consequences.

Levels of Performance

When the behavior child first starts your program, they should be at level one. In level one the child will go with you wherever you go, and be within an arm's length of you at all times. This means you stand at the door to the restroom while they use the facilities, and you take them to lunch. The child eats lunch in your behavior room and has no free time. The child should have a late-in-early-out plan for them in which they arrive at school an hour after it starts and leave an hour before it is dismissed. This reduces the chance that they will get into social situations. It will also give them a shorter day to cope with the idea of education and behavior. This entire ordeal lasts for about a month, or until the child reaches 30 days without a timeout. If the child does have a timeout, you go back to level one and start the 30 days over again.

Level two is where the child is allowed to go to recess and lunch by themselves. This is a lot of freedom for a behavior child and social situations like the recess and lunch room could get them in trouble. Let them think they are going by themselves, but keep a close eye on them. Inform the lunchroom and recess staff that your child is on the floor. Ask the staff to contact you as soon as they see anything that might get out of hand. You may want to do some personal observations to see if the student is getting along socially and that they are following school rules. If the child has a timeout during this level, go back to level one and start over again.

Level three is where the child is first mainstreamed into the special education class. If the child is learning disabled, they go into a special education class where the teachers receive training to handle learning disabled students' behaviors, and able to give the correct instruction for the appropriate grade level and ability. These classes are usually small and contain only a few other students. The students are able to maintain themselves while not being put placed into a crowd too soon. At level three, you need to stay in contact with the special education teachers so that you know exactly how your child is behaving and how they are dealing with confrontation.

Level four is for when the child should be able to become a part of a real mainstream class. The student will be either be unattended in the mainstream class or attend with a paraprofessional. It's always wise to have a paraprofessional to support the mainstream teacher when you have a behavior child in the class. The child will get behavioral support, and the paraprofessional will confront the child if they are showing any negative behavior. If the child is talking, the paraprofessional can say, "Stop talking." They will then give redirection. The child will accept a redirection or they will be pulled out of the classroom, taken for timeout, and then drop to level three.

The following levels are the same as the previous level, except that a new mainstream class will be added each 30 days the child behaves without a timeout. When the entire day is filled up with mainstream classes or special education classes and the child has been able to attend the full length of the educational day, they should be considered for release from the program. This is where you go into a 90-day period in which the child must have no timeouts while they are unsupported in the mainstream classes. This includes behavior on the playground, behavior at recess, behavior in PE, and behavior in the lunchroom. If any teacher confronts them and they are not accepting, they lose 90 days and go back to level seven.

Reward Systems

When beginning a reward system in the behavior classroom, you should start with small steps. You may consider giving a reward when a child behaves for an hour without being redirected. The rewards should be small things such as pencils, comic books, paperbacks, or other little trinkets you may have. Ask the child what kinds of things they like, you will then be able to stock those things in your sack and reward the student at the appropriate time. Some children will be happy with just a sticker or happy face, while others need a little more variety. Nobody works for free, not the teachers or the students, so keep that in mind when you are setting up a reward system. Everyone needs to get a positive return for doing something positive.

As the child's behavior improves, increase the hour time limit to maybe two hours. Increase the size of the prize also. Most special education children love food. Food is a great incentive, as long as you remember to keep it healthy. Boxes of raisins, dried fruit, trail mix, crackers, and juice boxes are a wonderful way to get even children in a high school behavior program to perform a task. Even if your school has a rule against food in the classroom, talk to your administration, letting them know what you are trying to achieve. Most administrative personnel will authorize you to do pretty much anything in the behavior classroom, as long as your kids behave and there are no unnecessary interruptions outside your classroom.

The next step is to try a half-day without redirection. This can be difficult for some kids, but at least they have already made some progress. You might want to come up with a plan to award points for every half-day without redirection. A full five days or five half-days without redirection should be enough to keep the child on the straight and narrow path. You can order a five-dollar pizza or begin a McDonald's reward for maintaining this long without redirection according to the point system you set for the classroom.

You will want to work toward a full day without redirection. Sometimes kids can be in your classroom for two or three years before they reach this point. If the kids can go five consecutive days without redirection, it's time for a big reward. A movie or a pizza party is a great incentive for the child. When the other children in the classroom who have not reached that same point see others get their own personal movie and a pizza, they may try harder to emulate the rewarded children the next time they have the opportunity. Personal time with the teacher may also be a good incentive. You can bring in McDonald's or other fast food that the child is not used to and have lunch one-on-one. This will allow you to develop a closer relationship with a child and allow you to tell a child what a good job they did.

Consequences

Every successful reward system should also have a consequence system. Consequences may be minor or major; according to what you decide to give the child as a result of the behavior or according to how the child perceives the consequence. One of the major consequences to a child is losing one of their levels. The child on the level system has to go back 30 days from the time he started for a timeout. This can be used as a threat or a promise when the child is on the second redirection. For example, if the child is on the second redirection and he looks like he is about to act out tell him that he would lose the progress (or level) he had worked for. You can even use words like, "Your mother and father would be very disappointed."

A minor consequence would be to lose a recess or lunch. If a child has to be redirected up to the second redirection many times every day, you have to make a decision on whether to punish the child for playing games. Sometimes the child will perform the same behavior throughout the day and only stop after the second redirection. This type of meddling with the system should be stopped as soon as it is recognized.

Consequences should be included in your behavior planning you provide to the parents. There is nothing like having a parent yell at you because their child received a consequence for something small. There are no small behaviors in the behavior classroom. If it goes against the rules, it is a behavior. The parent should know, well in advance, that the child is apt to get rewards for good behavior and will receive consequences whenever they misbehave. There should be no surprises for the parents when their young one comes home and tells them that they have gotten in trouble, lost a level, or have to spend lunchtime in the teacher's room.

One of the most effective consequences is the removal of the child during a fun activity in the room. If you're watching a movie, or playing a game with other children, they will naturally want to be a part of the activity. If they have been distracted most of the day and have not been on their best behavior, you should have your paraprofessional remove them from the room so they cannot participate. Sometimes this is the best way to give a child a consequence without having to drop a level or to hold them back during their socialization time during recess and lunch.

Share your consequences with your administration. Let them know what you plan to do when the child misbehaves. In the extreme case where a child refuses a timeout or has behavior that would harm them or other people, have a contingency plan so that you can take the child and keep them safe. Contingency plans are discussed in later chapters.

Have your consequences planned out and put them in rank, according to the severity of the behavior. You do not want to take away a recess for talking out loud in class, but you do want to take it away if a child talks out in class multiple times. You may even want to start a point system where the child can earn points during the day. If he misbehaves, points are taken away instead of turning them in for prizes or activity privileges. Time is a wonderful reward that doesn't cost any money. The child could turn his points in for free supervised time on the computer. Behavior children have a way of knowing the back doors to inappropriate websites which is why it is necessary to supervise them during this privilege.

Communication with Parents

As a behavior teacher you will have to stay in touch with parents more often than a mainstream teacher or a regular special education teacher. Sometimes the parents of a behavior child are needier than the child. You have to coordinate observations with what the parent has to say about medications, behaviors, and outside influences that may affect the child's behavior in the classroom.

The easiest line of communication is through e-mail. You can contact or reply to a message from the parent quickly. Some parents do not have a computer, so the next recourse is the telephone. A good rule-of-thumb is to contact a parent at least once a week. Ask if the child has had any medication changes or has any medical conditions that might inhibit their behavior for the upcoming week. Behavior children often have many medication changes and this causes them to act erratically or differently than they would normally behave. You should also ask the parent about any outside influences in the home that might affect the behavior. A death of a relative or friend might influence the behavior of the child in a dramatic way.

Some children that attend behavior programs in public schools have parents who are in prison. If the child receives a letter from the parent who is incarcerated, the child might act out in a way that is unsavory for the classroom, but through empathy you can understand what the child's going through. Many behavior children come from less than desirable home situations. These children were not taught how to act in a socially acceptable manner. Sometimes after meeting a parent you will understand why the child acts the way they do. Nurture over nature is the main cause of most problems with behaviorally challenged students.

A good way to give the parent what they need, in regard to information about the student, is in a weekly written report. This way, you will have a record that you did contact the parent. You will also have documentation if you are ever brought to trial because a parent says you did not communicate a behavior or problem to them. On this weekly report you should include grades, behaviors for the week, raising levels or lowering levels, rewards the child earned, and the consequences they received. This is the same information you may discussed on the telephone, but it is important to make sure that the parent has that information and you have a copy of the written document that you sent home. Remember, the behavior is the most important aspect of your job as a behavior teacher. Though academics are important, until a child learns to sit down and be on-task for a certain amount of time, he will not gain an understanding of any academic material that you prepare. So, the weekly report to the parent should include the academics, but the behavior should be stressed.

Some parents are open to you giving them advice on how to handle a child at home. Your student may be making great strides in school but on the home front they are slowly degenerating. Make sure that you word your feedback appropriately and do not give them a bias about the ways in which they can deal with the behaviors.

Communication with Outside Agencies

Not only does the behavior teacher have to communicate with parents, but they also need to communicate with outside agencies. Many of the students in a behavior program are members of a local group-home. They are placed outside of their home due to certain circumstances which affect the child in a negative way. The child may be in a group-home or in a foster family that has little to no experience with dealing with the behavior child.

Your communication should be directed to whoever the child is directly sponsored by. The local division of family services or mental health units will have a worker assigned to your child. Sometimes they have educational decision-making powers that are granted to them by the courts, but many do not. Before you release grades or any confidential material to these agencies, you must make sure that they have full educational rights for the child.

In addition to the other outside agency communications, the behavior teacher will sometimes deal with the court system. Oftentimes the teacher is called to represent the child, or the school, in reference to how the child is doing. The court system relies on teachers to be able to give a full academic and behavioral report to the court, which will then be compared with the behavior from the residential home, parents, or foster parents. With this information, the judge will make a decision to either place the child in an outside facility or to move the child closer for reunification of the family.

Your communication with the mental health agencies in your town is also very important. You generally have a child in your classroom for more than eight hours a day, and you have the closest thing to an observation report that these agencies can attain. Most health agencies will develop behavioral reports based on asking the child a specific series of questions. Sometimes the child will lie or be afraid to answer. When this occurs, the results are inconclusive and your input is needed to fill in the gaps of information on a child that might have been less than honest.

You should document all communications with parents, outside agencies, and even the discussions and e-mails between teachers. The behavior child is a volatile student who could very well be placed in the custody of a court at any time. Your input and your records of these documents must be kept so that you can back yourself up if you're ever implicated of wrongdoing or blamed for something that you did not do. All communications that you feel are important enough for the administration to see, you should provide a copy of the communication or at least keep in contact by e-mail with your concerns. Sometimes the agencies involved in these types of situations do not have the student's, school's or the teacher's well-being at heart.

Meetings

As a behavior teacher, you will go to more meetings than any other teacher or staff in the building, other than the administration. Not only do you attend annual IEP meetings, but many students need more meetings than once a year. As the student's behavior changes, so will his IEP. You may have three or more IEPs, per student, so these meetings require a lot of paperwork and even if you use the cut-and-paste method on a template for the IEP, the academic and behavior improvement are so fluid that you will need to change the IEP almost constantly.

Once the behavior changes, the child will begin to absorb their education rapidly. They will show more academic growth than a child who has been diagnosed with a learning disability. This rapid growth also causes a change in the levels at which the child will test. Many behavior children, once through the program, will be exited from special education. You have to be on top of your game to be able to catch the nuances which will help exit the child. This is especially important in the higher grades as a child matures and gets past puberty. As their behavior changes and social situations improve, they will realize that education and learning comes naturally to them. Most will have better grades and be able to be placed in higher classes.

Besides the IEP meetings, you usually have to attend the Multiple Disciplinary Team (MDT) meetings in which all parties that have an interest in the child will meet once a month to discuss improvement. These meetings usually include the caseworkers, teachers, Department of Family Service workers, mental health professionals, and any other person(s) who have had contact with the child. These meetings may last for an hour or more and are usually held after school.

Parents of children with behavior issues sometimes wish to meet with the teachers on a weekly or biweekly basis. Sometimes phone and e-mail communication is not enough to satisfy their desire to see that the child does better. These needs are sometimes met during your lunch, planning sessions or anytime that you have free before or after school. A good strategy for juggling time is to invite the parent to your classroom during lunch. You can each have a bite while discussing the child's behavior and you will not lose any time that you could be spending on other academic or non-teaching tasks.

Not only must you attend all the meetings that are associated with your work in the classroom, you also have to be present at all meetings other teachers are required to attend. This includes the monthly faculty meetings, department meetings, collaboration team meetings, and any other sort of meeting that might be added during the school year.

Collaboration meetings are usually held once a week. This is when a section of teachers come together and discusses strategies for learning. Even though most of the material in a collaborative meeting does not pertain to you, you can pick up some viable teaching strategies that will help with your children.

The monthly faculty meetings usually have a direct correlation to the monthly school board meetings. In the meeting, the principal or administrators will present what is going on with the district and how it will affect you. Other items on the agenda include school management and behavior management. Each of the subcommittees who are given a specific task to improve or change school culture will meet during faculty meetings to discuss ways to meet their goals and present their findings to you.

Another meeting that many teachers dislike is the annual standardized test meeting. Every school in the United States has to go through yearly testing to show the federal government or the state government that the school is measuring up to standards required of them. It takes anywhere from a week to three weeks out of your instructional year to administer these tests. Later chapters will discuss how to administer standardized tests to the behavior child.

A Reporting Agency

All teachers and public officials who work in a public school system are responsible to various reporting agencies. This means anything the student might say to you that would make you believe they had been physically abused, sexually abused, or their safety is at all compromised should be reported to your administration. In the behavior classroom this requires constant vigilance. Watch your children as they come into the room and prepare for class. Look for bruises or other marks on their arms, shoulders, or face that they cannot explain. Do not interrogate your student about where the bruises came from, but in a light-hearted manner try to get them to tell you what happened. The more your students trust you, the more they will respond to your questions.

If you discover a student that has unexplained bruises, or reports some harm that has happened at home, you need to contact your principal immediately and let them know the circumstances. Most schools have a program in which the school nurse will look at the child and a school counselor will talk to the child. This may upset the behavior child and he may refuse to speak. This is okay because if the incident is warranted, the Division of Family Services or the local authorities will come in and interview the child. If they determine the incident warrants a visit to the home, they will conduct it and see if any other actions need to be taken.

For example, if a student approaches you and says, "My dad got mad at me last night and pushed me up against the wall.", that is enough for you to make a report. Look for bruises on the child but do not touch the child in any manner. Then you should contact the administrator. To protect yourself, also send an e-mail to the administrator so that you have a record that you made the report. Do not be overzealous in the endeavors to find incidents, but be aware that abuse happens frequently to the behavior child.

You should be cautioned that behavior children often lie and manipulate to get their way. If their parent punished them before they came to school, or if they are angry with a parent in anyway, the behavior child will often lie or manipulate to get a parent into trouble. This may be just an outburst of emotion which the child cannot control, but it will set the wheels in motion for the authorities to check into what has happened.

Even if the accusation is false, the authorities may find other things that are unsavory or unsafe in the child's home. There was an incident in Wyoming where a child lied about the parent's abusiveness. It turned out that the parents were making methamphetamines in their bathtub. The parents were taken away and put in prison and the child was placed with a foster family. Even though the child was not physically or sexually abused, the environment in which the child lived was unsafe.

Remember that most behavior children come from a poor socioeconomic status. Most live in poor housing or income monitored housing. Even so, know that a small percentage of behavior children come from respectable homes with respectable parents. The majority of them come from parents who have little social skills themselves and continue the cycle of violence and abuse in the relationships they experienced as a child.

This presents an excellent opportunity for you to teach proper social skills in your classroom. Many young boys are abusive toward women and have learned the behavior from their parents. This hinders relationships with female teachers and school faculty. A good indication of the situation is when a student is mainstreamed and their negative behaviors are always present in a female teacher's classroom. The same can be opposite for a female student. If a female student has been abused by a male, they may be sheepish and shy with any male in the classroom. If they feel overwhelmed with emotion, they may even act out in the class and be sent to the office to get away from the male.

Unlike other teachers and school building personnel you are responsible for far more than just writing down grades and reporting the things you might see or hear. You must envelop yourself into the lives of the children that you teach. You need to know where they live, what their parents' names are and what their issues are. Be aware of what agencies are helping the family and what agencies are not. This is why the communication between parties is essential. The mental health caseworker might have information you need to put another piece into the puzzle and figure out what really went on a home.

The Behavior Child on Field Trips

Taking the behavior child out on excursions and field trips can be an exasperating experience for both the teacher and the student. Most behavior students do not know how to function outside the behavior classroom. Fortunately, they cannot be excluded from any activities in which they might maintain an acceptable global behavior. If your child is in a mainstream class and supported with a paraprofessional in that class, and the class is going on a field trip, you need to ensure that the paraprofessional can go along. You need to contact the parents and make sure that you not only have permission for the child to go, but you also need to have permission to pull the child from the activity and bring him back to the behavior classroom, if he misbehaves.

This takes some planning on your part. You need to make sure you have an emergency plan if you have to remove the child from a field trip. Most field trips are conducted with bus transportation. Have a paraprofessional ride on the bus with the child, but make sure they have a cell phone to call you to come get the child if the need arises. With this backup plan, you have to make sure the parents give you permission to transport the student in your personal vehicle. You should also get the administration's permission because you and the school district will be liable if you are involved in a car accident.

The best plan would be to have a small special education bus carry the child, or another vehicle can follow the main bus in case there is an emergency. This takes a lot of financial resources from the school district's budget, but as was stated before, it is the child's right to attend these functions if they can keep their behavior in check. If the child is at a museum, restaurant, or other site and they begin to act out; the child can immediately be taken from the group to an area where he can work through his emotions without causing a public disturbance.

The parents should be contacted immediately. Let them know the child was removed from the activity and that they may come pick the child up or you can use your backup transportation plan and have the bus, private vehicle, or other vehicle escort the student back to school. If the child becomes so out of control that a paraprofessional cannot handle him, the parents should be called and local law enforcement officers should be called to keep the child safe.

A behavior child should not be allowed to go on a field trip or out on a school excursion unless you are sure that he can maintain his behavior. Of course, there will be some exceptions in which the child will exhibit good behavior in the school setting, but will totally lose control of his/her behavior once he/she is outside the school building. This is associated with the behavior they may display at home but do not demonstrate at school. It is a good time for you to have some parent communication and find out what behavior the child expresses in a department store, grocery store, or another environment outside the school setting. The parents can give you enough information to help you make the decision about whether or not the child should be allowed to attend the field trip.

The Behavior Child and Sports

The behavior child has the right, unless it is excluded by the IEP, to attend after school functions and to join athletic teams. Most behavior children have a very hard time with competition. If your student does not take it well when he/she loses a board game or has a temper tantrum when he starts losing, then joining a sports team may not be the appropriate thing for him/her to do.

The prudent thing to do would be to put the child into a regular mainstream PE class. Watch the competition and the stress level as the child interacts with others. If he does well in the PE setting he might be ready for the next step. You can test the child with a simple game of one-on-one in basketball or just go outside and throw a baseball or football around. If the child is frustrated when they miss the ball or makes a bad throw, it could be a sign that he would not do well in a team environment.

If the child does decide to go out for the team, the coach and all adult personnel associated with the team needs to know the possibility of an anger outbursts or some showing emotionality. Let them know what to expect and how to deal with it. You might want to call a meeting with all the adults involved and have a contingency plan, if the child should act erratically or misbehave. This is especially important if the team goes on out-of-city athletic event to another school. The parents need to be involved in order for you to be able to pull the child back in if they act out during an athletic event. It could be very embarrassing for the school but worse, it could be emotionally disturbing for the child and the other students on the team.

As a behavior teacher, you might want to go with the child for the first couple of team events. Observe their behavior when the team is losing or when they make an unsuccessful play. Also observe the behavior if a child is not being allowed to play in the game very much. After the game, if everything goes well, process with the child and make sure the child understands that competition is about winning and losing. Give kudos for their good participation and confront them on what they did wrong. Develop strategies that will help the child understand how to behave more properly at the next event.

When a student is in the behavior program at the junior high and high school levels, their behavior will not just be scrutinized by you as a teacher. Everyone will watch the behavior on the playing field. Most of the time there are police officers or law enforcement personnel who will attend the events. The behavior child needs to know that if they are aggressive or break any laws during the course of play, they may be pulled from the game. If they are still not brought under control, they may be handed over to a law enforcement officer. Just because a child has a behavior problem they are involved in a behavior program does not mean they are allowed to go beyond the limits of social behavior or break the law. They need to understand this concept and the parents need to understand that the child will be arrested and charged for whatever offense they have committed.

The Behavior Child and After-School Activities

After-school activities are another venue in which the student of the behavior program might get into trouble. Many schools hold after-school programs such as homework club, social clubs, dances, and other social events. Again, unless the IEP states that your child cannot be a part of these functions, he/she will be allowed to go to them. Here is where your job as a behavior program facilitator comes into play.

The most important thing about after-school programs is that they are fun and full of social activity. Most behavior children cannot handle themselves in social situations and behaviors may erupt. If they are an older child, social situations like dating or going to a dance could crush them emotionally and cause more behaviors in the classroom on the following day.

You need to contact all adults involved with the after-school activities. Without breaking the bond of confidentiality, you need to let them know what behaviors to expect and what to do if these behaviors arise. After-school activity is funded and run by people other than teachers most of the time. Essentially you do not have any authority over what the child does in after-school programs.

The best thing that you can do is to inform all of the people involved, and let them know that behavior might become a problem during the activity. The communication really needs to be made available to the parent who is responsible for the child after the school day has ended. Let them know that they are fully responsible for their child's behavior and that the child will be placed under arrest by the authorities if he becomes out of control or harms another person. You may even want to have the parents sign a statement of accountability, as proof that they understand what will happen if the child does not behave.

The student should have the resources to call parents, family members, or other people who can help him out of the situation quickly. Without this failsafe in place, the child could be left emotionally distraught or have anger outbursts that could affect him socially for the rest of the school year. After-school programs need to be thoroughly thought out before a child is allowed to go to them. The administration needs to be notified and you need to document every communication you have with all parties involved so the results of the behavior do not come back and haunt you.

Most behavior children relish the chance to be part of normal social situations, but sometimes their minds and their personalities just cannot handle it. This is especially true in the junior high school arena. Junior high school students can be very emotional, and they are just beginning to experiment with boy and girl relationships. A misplaced note or a rumor floating around the school can destroy the child's self-esteem and set him back in your behavior program.

Giving Two Choices

When you are dealing with the behavior child, giving the child too many directions and choices at one time will usually cause them to shut down or take a long time to process the entire situation. The child will spend more time trying to figure out what the choices are than if you simply give the child two clear choices. When the child is good and there is an academic project going on, you can provide the two choices. One choice could be to do a crossword puzzle or another option would be to complete a worksheet. The child may immediately go for the one they think will be the least work, but you can set the standard by having the same work, only a different type of learning activity.

For example if you are doing multiplication and the child is ready for their math problems, you may tell him that he can do a multiplication grid sheet or 20 problems without a grid sheet. Most kids have the grid sheet down and have learned how to manipulate it so that they can just fill in the numbers up to seven and then give a lot of effort from seven to nine. So of course, offer the grid sheet first. You use a grid sheet as a learning tool. Even though the kids think they are manipulating the system by filling in the numbers, they are actually learning the facts and the same combination of sequences of numbers will give them a better foundation for using a multiplication grid later on.

After the break time is completed, it is time for the next assignment. Bring out the original sheet the child did not want to complete and also one that is a little more difficult and more than likely the child will decide to reject it. It is logical that they will choose the sheet that you had put out the first time and they thought was more difficult, while in reality they are completing the original assignment. At the same time they are thinking that they are getting their way because they have made a decision between two choices.

When the child exhibits negative behavior, you can use the two choice methods in a peripheral way. For example, the child is in the timeout room and already processed but he still has time remaining in your class before he can proceed. Always make sure there are academic choices after a negative behavior. You may give him instruction to read his library book for 20 minutes, or you can give him the choice of writing an essay about what they did wrong. Of course the child will choose the library book. If you have the original intent that you want the child to be quiet and to think about his problems, giving him a horror story that you know he will not want to read, means he will choose to work on the assignment you want him to complete.

In the two choice methods, the only negative thing that comes out of it is when the child refuses to do either option. First of all, refusal is not allowed in the behavior classroom. After you use the redirection process and the child still refuses necessary direction, they should be sent to the timeout room. After a timeout and processing, give them the same two choices. It may seem an endless battle of refusal and timeouts which may last hours until the child is tired of sitting in an empty room and is ready to comply with the rules.

Two choices can be used for almost anything that you do in the classroom, even with fun things that you planned to give the students, such as a break. You can give them a choice of working on a puzzle or playing a board game. The child who is very shy will choose to do the puzzle and the more extroverted child will be up for playing a board game. With this system, you can manipulate fun time as well as assigned material. The children are aware of what relaxes them. Some of them like to color, and some like to do puzzles, some of them like to write and internalize, and yet others like to play war games and socialize. During these moments, you can actually discover more about the child's personality and find out if they are an introvert or an extrovert.

Reducing Work in the Behavior Classroom

Most of your students will have either ADHD or other emotional distress which will causes a lack of concentration on any given piece of work at one time. This can cause the child to be overly anxious and sometimes act out to avoid the work. When the child first comes to the behavior classroom you need to look at what they can do before the behavior starts. Begin with approximately five minutes of work. This can be accomplished with flashcards, worksheets, or even by building a house or playing a game. See how long that child can concentrate on one thing without acting out or being distracted. When you have determined the amount of time, you need to increase it slowly by a minute each day. Between the times that the child does work the breaks should also be decreased.

For example, if you start the child on five minutes, you might give a ten minute break for five minutes of work. The next day you might want to try six minutes of work with a ten minute break. This would seem like you're giving more break but when you reach the 30 minute mark, you will need to start cutting back the break time. This can be accomplished when the child knows that he has done so well at the work, that it will be made a part of a consequence and reward system. So when the child works constantly for 30 minutes, they may come up and receive 30 minutes of break time. After he has accomplished the first 30 minutes, schedule 31 minutes of work and 29 minutes of break time. Slowly decrease the amount of time until you are able to hold a regular class with the appropriate amount of break time the child needs.

You have to realize that this is a slow process and behaviors may rise, therefore you may have to struggle through the process all over again. The best resource to help with this problem is just to be patient and document everything you've done. Some kids will sabotage themselves and continuously go back to the 5/5 method, but little do they realize that the 5/5 method is still 30 minutes of work and 30 minutes of break time. You have to remember that the break time is important for the behavior child because it can be used as a reward.

Another strategy is to use a break time as a long-term reward. With this strategy, you would use it when the work session is successful. After the bell goes off and you have been working for five minutes and the child is still involved with the project, Look at the child and tell them if they continue working for another five minutes you will write down (on an index card) that they have a five-minute of any time off free pass. This means that the child can use the card any time they want to stop what they are doing and have a five-minute free time. This can be abused and will sometimes be used as an avoidance measure for doing something they do not like to do, such as math or reading. It is fine if the child says, "I want to take my 20 minute free break during reading." You tell them, "Sure, that is okay, but this is the choice that you are making." The child needs to know that reading is important and that if it is done now, it will be out of the way later on. Also remind the child that they may want to use the card later on when there is a really bad assignment or when they are frustrated.

Regardless of how you use the timeout strategy for reducing the time of on-task work, you as a teacher need to be flexible. Do not let the child try to manipulate you to try to get more time. Do not fall for batting eyelashes or big sad eyes. The children know what they are doing and often want to leave the work until the last minute, rather than completing it in a timely manner. Explain to the child that each individual works at their own pace, that it is a unique business, and that they are getting a reward for being successful, at their own pace, within the class. You are the one who is in control. Explain to the child what you are doing and why you are doing it.

Videotaping the Behavior in the Behavior Classroom

When you have a student that has very bizarre or violent behavior, you may want to get permission to videotape that behavior. You need the permission of both the parents and the administration to use this technique and record the child's behavior at its worst. A child may act worse in your behavior classroom than they do at home and some parents cannot believe their child can be overly aggressive or angry. Once you have permission, put the camera in the corner of a room, higher than your kids can reach. You may want to focus the camera toward a behavior room door and be able to redirect it or have it taken down by a paraprofessional while the behavior is going on. This way you can record the behaviors of the child in a worst case scenario and give the parent a videotape representation of the child's behavior.

The children's behavior can be predicted after you have been around them for a while and have used a video camera as a deterrent to aggressive or violent behavior. You simply tell a child what you expect of them, then walk over and turn the camera on and then walk back and confront the child. Sometimes the threat of being recorded will be enough to restrain the child from going beyond the limits of your classroom rules. The likelihood of violent behavior that would have gotten them thrown out of the program will be reduced.

Videotaping may be an extreme measure, but it will give you protection in court if the parents decide to sue you. In very extreme cases, some parents will use their child's behavior as a wedge to sue the school district or the state. Many parents are savvy about how to manipulate the situation, but you have nothing to worry about if you document the way you appropriately handle yourself and their child's behaviors. Watch out for this legal nightmare that can ruin your career or at least give you a bad mark, even though you probably handled the situation correctly.

After you videotape a child, you need to take out the videotape from the recorder and put it in a safe and secure place. Never record another's child's behavior on the same tape as the child that you are intending to videotape. It can be very embarrassing in court and could be against confidentiality laws when another child's behaviors are shown, even for a minute, in your filming process. Focus on the child and the person confronting the child. Do not pan around the room and get other people's faces in the videotaping. If you do happen to get another student's face in the videotaping and you are going to use that videotape to defend yourself in court, then you need written permission for that child's face to be shown in a court room.

The bottom line is that videotaping students as protection works not only for the students, but also protects you. You are probably the only one in the room with the child when disturbances happen. If the paraprofessional is in the room, they can film, otherwise you need to position yourself in an area in front of the camera so that the behavior will be displayed and not be off-camera. Also turn on the volume so that the voices record, in case a child is using expletives or is being verbally aggressive.

Accepting "No as an Answer"

One of the most difficult things for a behavior challenged child to do is to accept "no" as an answer. This may be due to the child's past experiences in the classroom or because their parents coddled the child, giving into their whims. Not being able to accept the word "no" in the classroom or from any adult is a serious problem for these unfortunate children. They will try to manipulate and get their way or no matter what. They may cry or whine or go into more extreme measures such as holding their breath or throwing a tantrum.

As a behavior teacher, you need to stand your ground when it comes to your students and the word "no". It should be the number one behavior modification that you try to achieve with the child from the first time you meet them until they leave your program. The behavior child will try anything to get their way and you will have to let them know that they are not going to get their way.

When the behavior child gets "no" as an answer they will either whine or they will make a negative comment. You need to stop them in their tracks when they do this. You need to let the child know that they are overstepping their bounds and operating against one of the behavior classroom rules. Tell the child to stop immediately. You do not have to say anything else but "stop". After the child has your full attention you can tell them it is their responsibilities as a student to accept "no" as an answer.

The student may react in two ways. They may recognize that they have broken one of the rules and will stand there silently waiting for you to reprimanded them or they will continue the behavior or even escalate it into a more undesirable situation. Not all but some of these children are from families that cater to their wishes and will let them have what they want so they will not make a fuss about it. Even though they may get their way at home it is your job as a teacher to make them understand they must behave appropriately in school so that they can get through your program.

Even though saying "no" to a behavior child is sometimes hard, the child needs to learn that they will have to be said "no" to on countless occasions throughout their lives. You are providing a lifelong lesson of how to accept something that they do not want to accept. You will also teach the child that they will not be able to force their will on you or any other adult. You are not taking their will but you are giving them a skill that they will need at home and in relationships, the social system, in the workplace, and almost every situation that they might themselves in during their lifetime.

Accepting the responsibility for not getting their way it is one of the most important lessons that the behavior child can learn. If they learn this and nothing else in your classroom, you have done your job as a teacher and set them up, at least in a primitive way, for all life's challenges in the future. They will be told "no" all their lives and they must be able to accept "no" as an answer and they will be able to exert their communication when the behavior child says "no" to others.

Accepting Criticism or Critique and the Behavior Classroom

One of the hardest things for a behavior child to do is accept criticism or critique about their work, their appearance, or the way they are behaving. Some children will act as though you have plunged a knife into their heart if you give them any negative criticism at all. When you approach a behavior child, you need to approach them with kid gloves and let them know what they are doing is wrong (academically) but do so in a way in which you let them know that it is okay to be wrong and it is okay to have a wrong answer occasionally.

Some behavior children wear their feelings on their sleeve and will manipulate you by attempting to stop you from giving those negative critiques or criticism. They will whine and cry so that you will feel bad about your criticism and stop giving it to them. Everything a behavior teacher does with the behavior child, the behavior teacher has to stand their ground. Let them know that even though the work may be good for now, it could be better, because they are capable of doing better. Do not cushion the criticism or critique and let the behavior student know the criticism is a part of life and they need to accept it.

You might want to roll play with your paraprofessional or another student in your classroom to let them know how to accept criticism graciously. One of the hardest things, even for an adult, to do is to accept feedback that is negative or might be contrary to what they believe is right. Show the child when they have made an error, and tell them how this could be an easy mistake and provide the steps to solve the problem. Offer a possible reason for the error that will make them accept their mistake.

Once the behavior child learns to accept criticism, they will be less apt to criticize others in a classroom. Most behavior children will insult other children and will make fun of other kids. This is why they must learn to accept criticism from others and give criticism, without hurting feelings. This may be very hard for the younger student, but as the behavior student grows older, they will realize that it is an embarrassing situation and maybe, just maybe, empathy might arise.

The behavior child will learn to accept criticism more once they realize that the criticism leads to more successes and they will begin to seek out criticism so that they may improve. By this time, if the child is dealing with criticism properly, they may be ready to graduate from your program and move on to mainstream classes, and be more successful than they were when they first began your program.

Even if a child does not need to be criticized or critiqued, take time and search out your day to find something wrong. They need the practice to learn how to accept the criticism and how to do so graciously. If you pick out the little things first, even though they are not doing anything larger, you may save them time and embarrassment later on.

Disagreeing Appropriately In the Behavior Classroom

In the behavior classroom there are going to be disagreements on a daily, if not hourly, timeframe. The behavior child is often defiant and will not only disagree with you, because they do not believe what you are saying, but they will also disagree just to be defiant and want to play games. As a behavior teacher you cannot stand for this. A child must understand that they have to disagree appropriately or they have no stand in the argument.

The behavior child may become upset if they think that you have given them a wrong answer or wrong direction. The proper way for the behavior child to disagree with an adult is to wait for the adult to stop talking and then tell the adult that they respectively disagree with what they have been told. The child is then allowed to tell the adult why they think. The adult has a chance to either respect the opinion of the student or in the case of the student that is being defiant, explain to the child that they respect their opinion but they are incorrect.

The behavior child may become very resistant to disagreeing in an appropriate manner. In their own life they may live in a world of argument and strife as parents, siblings, and other adults around disagree on many things that are a part of daily life. It is a learned behavior to argue and if they are not taught better ways of communication they will continue to disagree inappropriately and this will lead to strife within your classroom and in your own relationship with the child.

If you work with a behavior student for awhile you will learn that they will still try to test you on a disagreement. As you work with older students and their verbal defiance, you will find that an inappropriate argument is more common. You will find that they will try to manipulate you into an argument to gain control. Remember that you are the adult and you should be in control of the situation. When the child is not agreeing with you, this is a prime chance for you to test their limits of what behavior they have learned in your classroom. You can push the child into a disagreement and see how much control they have and how much they can restrain from argument.

This may not be the agreed upon method of teaching children, but it is a way to assess how the child might handle social situations outside your room. When a child constantly argues it may be a sign of conduct disorder and the verbal defiance is a symptom of something larger than it is out of your control. Sometimes this argument scenario may be gender-based and the child may be more argumentative toward males than females or vice versa.

As in all situations in the behavior classroom, you as the behavior teacher need to be in control of the conversation, the disagreement, and the final outcome of the communication. This is an opportunity for you to teach a viable life lesson about arguing and social communication and you will be able to teach the child how to disagree appropriately without becoming a social outcast.

Seeking the Teacher's Attention in the Behavior Classroom

The simple act of raising a hand and getting the teachers attention is a difficult thing for the behavior student. Most behavior students are impulsive and will blurt out an answer or ask for help without raising a hand. They will yell across the room or act in an inappropriate manner to gain the teachers attention. If the behavior child is going to be mainstreamed into regular classes, they need to have good skills to gain the teachers attention, without causing a classroom disruption or drawing attention to themselves.

The behavior teacher needs to enforce a hand raising rule in the behavior classroom. The skill needs to be recognized as a behavior and the child should be given rewards or consequences in accordance to the adherents to this behavior. If the child tries to gain the behavior teacher's attention inside the behavior classroom without raising their hand, the behavior teacher has a right to redirect them toward the proper behavior. This may take several times of explaining to the student that by raising their hand continuously, the behavior teacher may see them but may not be able to get to them immediately.

A simple solution for this in the behavior classroom is to have a non-physical type of signal such as asking the teacher to come to the desk to help. This could be arranged by placing flags at the end of the table or by raising up a predetermined object, so the teacher can see that the object is erect and that the student needs the teacher's attention. The biggest problem with the raising of the hand is that students in the behavior classroom often do not have the patience to wait. Even if the teacher gives them a nonverbal gesture that they will be there as soon as possible, the behavior student will continue to stretch their arm, grunt, or make noise to get the attention immediately.

The behavior student may exhibit center-of-attention, behavior that directs the attention toward them even if it distracts the other students in the room. If the child exhibits this kind of behavior, the teacher may purposely not go to the child, in order to see how they will react. Redirect the child and give only nonverbal signals that you will be there in a second, but stay away for awhile and see how long it will take before the student realizes that they are not the center of attention. This will give you a good guideline to gauge the behavior and that you need to correct the behavior.

This behavior needs to be stopped before the child goes into a mainstream class. Not only will the student become a distraction for other students but it will become a nightmare for the teachers trying to teach the class. There are already enough needy, non-special education students in the class that have a problem gaining the teacher's attention. Adding a child into any mainstream class that does not have the proper skills to seek a teacher's attention will add chaos to a normally serene classroom.

When to Use a Loud Voice

The behaviors of your child will dictate when a child needs to be reprimanded verbally. If a child is totally out of control and is in danger of hurting themselves or others, you might choose to use a loud voice to stop the behaviors. A loud, "Stop!" will usually stop the child in their tracks and force them to give you some attention. A loud voice may stop the child if they are in range or if they are out of control and have lost their temper. You have to choose the time and place to use a loud voice; otherwise, you might do more damage than good.

Loud voice used in the behavior room will not only affect the job with the behavior, but it may also affect the behavior and emotions of the other children in the room. Some of these children may come from a damaged home in which there is fighting an inordinate amount of the time. A loud voice will take them out of their safe place and put them into a state of fear or shock. Make sure that when you use a loud voice, it is only to stop a behavior that is hurting the academic environment of your room or the safety of a peer.

If there is an argument between students explodes into a fight in your room, you cannot touch the children and you should not put them in the timeout room. If two children are fighting, step between them and say in a loud voice "Stop fighting". Most kids in the middle school age range will comply immediately. If it is a fight with high school age children, then you should not step between them but call for help immediately.

When you have total chaos in your room, using a loud voice may be the only way for you to bring your room back under control. The children respect authority and using a loud voice to get their attention might be the method that you choose. The behavior child will sometimes jump or even have a breakdown when loud noises are used, so you have to use it sparingly. Sometimes, just lowering your voice and talking slower is better than a loud voice. Be sure that you know your children well, and what voice to use and on what occasion. If you are getting angry or feel that you are getting out of control yourself, walk out of the room, and take a deep breath before going back in.

Following Instructions in the Behavior Classroom

For the behavior child to be successful in the main stream classroom, they need to learn how to follow instructions. Following directives not only needs to be adhered to verbally but also with the written word. The child needs to take on the responsibility of listening to instructions and when they are reading them but they need to learn how to follow them completely. Without this essential skill the child will not be able to find employment later in life nor will they be able to function in mainstream society.

If your behavior child has difficulty following instructions, you as a behavior teacher will need to be able to take a multiple step instruction and turn it into little chunks in which the behavior child can absorb. If the instructions are in a paragraph form you might be able to put numbers in front of the steps inside the paragraphs or cut the sentences out of the instructions so that the child may see little pieces of direction instead of being overwhelmed.

When you have the behavior child who cannot follow instructions, you can write the first instruction on an index card or on the board and have the child follow through with this instruction without too much difficulty. Once the first instruction is completed, the teacher should take away the index card or erase the white board and place the next instruction on it. If you have more than one behavior child in the room, you may want to use index cards because if you take away the first instruction while others are working on it, it may cause mass confusion.

Once the child has a working idea of how directions work, you can move on to helping them understand them in the mainstream classroom. In the mainstream classroom, things go faster and they can become confused very easily. If the instructions are verbal, have the paraprofessional or yourself sit behind the child and write down the instructions the teacher is explaining, once you have the instructions written down. You can approach the child individually and let them follow the instructions one at a time.

If the child is taking a test, you or the paraprofessional may need to cover up a part of a test with a white sheet of paper so that the child will not be overwhelmed by words on the whole page and can concentrate on the instructions first. Sometimes following the instructions is harder than answering the questions. If a child sees questions they know they can answer, they will skip the instructions and haphazardly start to answer the questions in the test. Most of the time this will be wrong and if the child is very bright they may be able to proceed without reading the instructions.

If the child is reluctant to follow instructions the behavior teacher needs to redirect the child so that they will understand that it is a behavior that can be changed. If they refuse to follow instructions or become frustrated when given instructions, the teacher needs to take the child out of the room and follow the behavior plan implemented upon the child. Remember that some behavior children are also learning disabled and you will need to approach each student differently and give them modifications in a way they can process without having an emotional display.

Staying On Task in the Behavior Classroom

Many emotionally disturbed children or behaviorally challenged children have a hard time staying on task. This is either because of ADHD or because of the medications that they are on. They are easily distracted and will look for anything to take them off task. As the behavior teacher you need to teach the child how to stay on task and not let outside distractions sidetrack them from the work. This can be extremely hard for some children and you have to be patient and constantly monitor the child's behavior during challenging activities.

The behavior child will not only be off task but will purposefully use bad behavior to get into trouble so they do not have to complete the task. This is a manipulation that you should be aware of and recognize, in order to stop the behavior at the first possible moment. Putting the behavior child in an enclosed area where they cannot see other distractions is just a Band-Aid on the issues that the child is attempting to avoid. If you have a child that is having a hard time staying on task, let them stay on task for just one or two minutes. Reward them if they can stay focused through the agreed-upon time and be able to complete the task after a series of breaks and work time.

On task behaviors become more manageable when you allow the child to get a reward for extended time. Have the child try for five minutes instead of the two or three that they began with. As time goes by, and the student matures, you will discover that off task behavior will be less apparent and you will have to use less rewards or consequences for a child to get on task and stay on task. You may even monitor them on a leisure activity, such as pleasure reading. You can time them on how long that they can stay on task. If you find out that the child can sit and read a book for 10 or 20 minutes without being off task, then you know that their behavior is more than likely a manipulation when they stay off task during the assignment they do not like.

Most behavior students understand what they are doing when they demonstrate off task behavior. Some students will stare off into space and when you confront them, they will look at you like they were staring off into space purposefully. This is a manipulation so that you will confront them, and the confrontation takes them off task. Some kids will use the spacing out method as a crutch when they think that they can get away with it. Stand firm and do not let them get away with off task behavior. Recognize the behavior and tell the child that being off task is an unacceptable behavior and that they need to be on task for a specific amount of time.

If a child does not remain on task even after prompting, you need to use classroom redirection procedure. Redirect them and give them a choice of a voluntary timeout or lead them back on task. They may pretend to be on task for just a few minutes, but watch them closely because if they exhibit the same behavior within a few minutes, they need to be redirected and possibly placed into a mandatory timeout. Watch their eye movements. Some students just want the opportunity to look around the room when you're not watching them or try to talk to another student. The more they see the eyes of others, the more your eyes need to be upon them. They know what you are doing and how you will react and they will challenge you every chance they get.

Dealing with the Behavior of Rambling

Sometimes it is difficult to teach the behavior student because the student has a specific behavior they display when they are being taught. One specific behavior that many teachers have to deal with is rambling. This is where a student wanders off subject and uses inappropriate analogies or examples in an attempt to get the question right. Rambling should not be allowed in the behavior classroom because the child uses this behavior to get off task or to redirect the instruction to something they want to talk about. Once the action is seen as a behavior, rambling needs to be addressed as a negative behavior.

To end rambling, you need to refocus the child on the subject at hand. Ask them to stop talking and let them know you appreciate the input, but do not let them ramble on taking up valuable academic time. You can refocus the child by letting them know that they are getting off task or by restating the question that started their rant. Once they see that they are being dealt with for rambling, most will redirect to the subject matter. Very shrewd children will turn their rambling around to a new twist to keep the instruction off task.

You may want to ask the child to tell you why what they are saying is related to what is being said. It may not be a behavior and the child simply has the wrong idea in their head. You can use this a mini-educational side line moment to explain how what they were talking about and the subject at hand are totally different. This might take some "out of the box" or critical thinking skills, but if worded right, it could be a wonderful educational experience for the child. Sometimes mini-lessons off the subject are received more than the actual material.

Another way to pull the rambling child around to your side of the conversation is to use visual aids. Just step back from the interaction between yourself and the child and turn your back and begin to write on the board or set up another form of visual aid. The distraction through movement may be enough for them to stop the behavior to watch what is going on. If the visual aid does not distract or refocus the child, you will have to use behavior room redirection to get them off their rambling.

Asking for Permission in the Behavior Classroom

In the behavior classroom, the behavior student has a hard time asking for permission. They are very impulsive and they want to have their way now and then. As a behavior teacher, you have to be able to recognize this problem and teach the proper way to ask permission. Whether it is to go to the bathroom or to get up and sharpen their pencil, the behavior child needs to understand what the parameters are when it comes to asking to do something or needing attention or help. Your room and your program have to have certain guidelines to help the child understand and follow what you need as a behavior teacher.

The first thing you need to do, as a behavior teacher, is to establish a signal plan when a child wants to ask permission. A normal procedure is to raise the hand. This is what is done in other classes and this is what should be taught in classroom. Have the child raise their hand when they need permission to do something instead of yelling out, waving their hand about or do anything at all, other than having their hand raised. Once you recognize the child you can either walk over to them or give the child a nonverbal signal that you have seen them. At this point, the child should be taught to lower the hand until you can give them your undivided attention.

When your child goes to a mainstream classroom, make sure that this proper behavior goes with them. Let the mainstream classroom teacher know that this is the expected behavior of your student and that the student should adhere to your wishes. In some incidences, if the child is left alone in a mainstream classroom, the child will revert back to old ways or try to challenge the new teacher. This should not be tolerated. This behavior must be confronted and if not redirected, consequences should follow.

The activities for which permission needs to be granted should be decided by the teacher. The behavior teacher should make allowances for emergencies such as going to the bathroom, if the child has bathroom issues. Even simple tasks such as sharpening pencils or taking a book off the shelf should have boundaries placed upon them. The student should always get permission from the teacher to leave the room or talk to another student.

Listening To Music in the Behavior Classroom

A behavior student has a difficult time listening to instructions. In order for the student to get the best academic support, you must keep noise levels low inside the behavior classroom. The teacher should make sure the classroom is quiet at all times. There should be no distractions whatsoever, and the student should be able to hear everything that is said. The littlest noise can distract the behavior student and even the gurgling of a fish tank or the closing of a door can bring them off task. The child must have a total silence to be able to focus on the work.

For older students, music is a good way to give ambient sounds to the background and let the child concentrate on their work. In most schools, CDs, MP3 players, and other listening devices are banned. This does not work in the behavior classroom, for the older student. Let the student play their own music and if they are comfortable working in that environment then allow them to continue. Music is a great way to let the student feel like they have some ownership of their study time and at the same time the music is kept to a level where only they can hear it.

Do not get into a battle with your behavior student about music. Though you might think that some of their music is inappropriate, remember that it is the students who are listening to it and their parents probably approve of it. If a behavior child is not playing their own music at school, then it would be okay for you to play music from a CD player or computer in your room. Easy listening is not a good choice. If the child knows the words to the music they will hum or sing-along. The best music for the behavior classroom is New Age sounds which have a rhythm and a beat that is not easy to keep time to.

You can also use music to reward the child. If the child is going through some difficulties and needs a timeout that is not mandatory, let them take their listening device to the timeout room so they can simply sit and relax for a while. Music is known to calm some of the most aggressive behaviors and if you let that be a reward, it is another good tool in your toolbox for managing your behavior classroom. Have strict rules about music and do not let it get out of hand. Music is another way children can manipulate you and if they do you can use it as a consequence instead of a reward.

Implementing a Behavior Intervention Plan

A Behavior Intervention Plan (BIP) is essential for special needs students in any educational environment. Having this plan in place can make a big difference in how special needs students react to and act within their school environment. The plan is useful for the student and education professionals as it is instrumental for encouraging all participants to work together. The process can be long and frustrating and requires the cooperation and enthusiasm of the appropriate school personnel. One way to speed up the process is to develop a plan of your own to present to education providers. Of course, it will be necessary to have a good relationship with your child study team, teachers and other school personnel. At the very least, your plan will provide a starting point from which to build a comprehensive plan that incorporates all the participants' perspectives.

Step 1 – Conduct a Functional Behavioral Assessment
The first step in developing the BIP is to conduct a Functional Behavioral Assessment (FBA), which is an attempt to investigate the child's behavior, rather than simply classify an act as a bad behavior. Many times behaviors are misinterpreted as "bad" rather than seen as a tool used by the child to serve a particular need or function. Understanding what is motivating a child to behave in a negative manner is the key function of the FBA. Once it is understood why a child behaves the way they do, strategies can be developed to stop or modify their behavior.

Step 2 – Ensure the quality of the Functional Behavioral Assessment
Educational institutions are required by law to conduct a comprehensive FBA in relation to special needs students with challenging behaviors. Even though this is a legal requirement, sometimes a parent has to initiate this exercise and push the process through to completion. It is important that the parent does not accept blanket type answers or assessments but is satisfied that the conclusions drawn coincide with the needs of the particular child and their behaviors. The technique to develop an effective FBA, is to observe, identify and document the activity, action, environment, behavior, etc., that precedes the negative behavior and then observe and document what the child does after the behavior or consequence. This is conducted over several weeks through discussions with teachers, parents and others who have contact with the child.

Step 3 – Functional Behavioral Assessment Evaluation
Once the FBA is compiled, the next step is to look at the behaviors in relation to the precursor and the consequence in order to draw conclusions about the child's condition and reaction to their environment. After the conclusions are drawn and agreed on by the parents, teachers, and others who have contact with the child need to determine how the child's environment can be changed and find ways to remove the reason for the negative behavior.

Step 4 – Develop the Behavior Intervention Plan
A BIP translates the observations, conclusions and evaluations of the FBA to develop a foundational plan to use in managing the child's behavior. This plan is used by all participants including, but not limited to, the child, parents, educators and other school personnel.

The BIP should include:
   a. Actions needed to change the environment that will preempt the negative behavior.
   b. Give examples of positive reinforcements that can be used to encourage good behaviors.
   c. The use of predetermined techniques that can be used to ignore or avoid reinforcing negative behaviors.

d. Provide options for use by team members so that the child will not be driven or tempted to act negatively due to frustration or exhaustion.

Step 5 – Implement the Behavior Intervention Plan
When all team members have agreed on the BIP, it is crucial that it be followed, with all parties understanding their level of obligation. All school officials are obligated by law to follow the plan, but it may take parent persuasion and intervention to ensure the plan is being followed as agreed upon and the negative results of diversions from the BIP are not being taken out on the child.

Work Completion for the Behavior Student

Work completion in the behavior class is one of the most challenging for the behavior student and involves their academic career. The behavior student is almost always off task and passionately hates to do schoolwork. Work completion can cause emotions to rise and the behaviors to manifest. To teach behavior work completion skills, the behavior classroom teacher should start small until they are comfortable with the amount of work the student is doing.

The best way is to start out small and provide the child with something you know they can complete in a given amount of time. Make the task something simple and when the child has completed it praise them. The child needs to have a sense of accomplishment and learn what it is to feel their job is completed. As the time goes on, add a little bit more to the task, challenging the child. There may be some resistance to more work being added, but if you do so in a careful manner, the child will understand that you are challenging them and they need to comply. Every time a child completes the work on time, give them a reward, or at least a verbal reward stating that they did the right thing.

You may even want to try to work with the parents and have them assist with the work completion behavior also. If the child is struggling with chores or with completing homework at night, maybe the parents can set something up with you at school so the child can be rewarded and they can gain points by completing jobs and tasks at home.

You might be able to set the child up with a job completion chart. This will give the child a visual aid of where they need to be and what to do next. You could even use a learning contract in which the child can see the extent of the task in front of them and be able to check off each of the items as they are completed. Even something as simple as reading a number of pages in a given time will give the child a goal and a sense of satisfaction when the task is completed. You can assign the child 10 pages of a book and then check off a box that reads, "10 pages are completed." The next week you may want to jump up to 11 pages. This way the child understands what they are to do and how it feels to get the job done and done right.

The Behavior Chart in the Classroom

Some behavior children are visual learners and prefer to see their academic and behavior scores posted. A behavior chart is a great way to graph behavior, whether it is on a daily, weekly, or monthly basis. These children will be able to see where they were at one time and where they have slipped up.

You can use pretty much any design to your behavior chart, but a necessity is to keep the age of the child in mind while you are designing it. You might want to design the behavior chart with more pictures and colors for a young child or a more refined behavior chart for the more mature student. Do not underestimate the maturity level by giving an older student stars and pictures on their behavior chart. That would only demean them and make them resistant to the chart.

The behavior child needs to know the assignment's progress, whether on the hourly or monthly basis, their efforts will be rewarded. They can take the chart home to show their parents. You may want to check the behavior chart and see if it is the right match for your child by determining how much you expect the child to achieve, in a certain amount of time, and whether they can actually attain it. The behavior child loves to see improvement, but at the same time, they may be depressed or their behavior may worsen after they view their chart.

If you are teaching a high-level math child, you may want to incorporate a math lesson into the formation of the behavior chart. Let the child have some ownership. If you want to teach them some computer skills, you can have them make a graph, pie chart, scatter chart, or other type of visual representation of the behavior.

This behavior chart can be sent home to the parents and act as a guide in the two-way communication between you and the parents, in regard to the behavior progress. The behavior chart is also an excellent source of information to have at an IEP meeting. You can use the graphics to show improvement or slight downfalls. It will be a comfort for the parent to see that your program is actually working. You can also show a child's diminishing behavior if the chart shows that, in a new environment, the child has regressed.

Dealing With Shyness in the Behavior Classroom

Not all behavior children act out. The introverted student also needs help through the day to deal with their emotions and their social awkwardness. Just as with the acting out child, the shy child needs special techniques to get them to come out of their shell and participate in class or group activities. The shy child should be encouraged and rewarded by showing extravert behavior and participating in the class activities. Reward them for even the littlest behavior that is away from their normal world of isolation.

If the child is struggling during group instruction, you may want to change the activity to more individual direction. This will allow the shy child be able to get back into their comfort zone without singling out the child and causing a negative emotional reaction. The child will be able to work on the concept and will not have the added burden of dealing with group interaction. Group work can be added as the child becomes more accustomed to what group interactions are about and how they can become a part of it comfortably. In time the child will slowly feel more comfortable and will be able to increase participation.

When you talk to the shy child, always give them eye contact and make sure that they do the same with you. Eye contact is very important whenever you talk to any of your students. By not giving eye contact, the child is escaping the personal interaction that they want to avoid. Stop what you are doing and look the child in the eye and let them know that this is the proper way for people to act when they are talking to each other. The eye contact will happen as the child trusts you more, but be diligent and make sure that they are giving eye contact to other people when they are spoken to.

As the shy child becomes more comfortable, try new strategies to bring them into the fold. Once they have gained your trust, try to get them to share that trust with another adult or a peer. There will always be some sort of shyness happening around groups, but with patience, trust, and persistence, the introvert may not become an extravert but they will be closer to a more stable public life. Shyness is a behavior, but one that can be overcome with time.

Testing Referrals

No matter what kind of behavior room you teach in, you need to have some criteria for entry into your program. Most behavior classrooms are designated for emotionally disabled children. This can be a simple baseline that will keep the oppositional defiant and the behaviorally challenged child out of your behavior classroom. You may also have a program that directly assists the behaviorally challenged or the oppositional defiant, and the emotionally disturbed or the emotionally disabled may not fit. ODD and ED children do not mix well in the classroom.

You have to have some control over the personality and the atmosphere that your classroom will have. One oppositional defiant child may interfere with the learning of many of the ED students enrolled. Defiance and open anger may make your ED students struggle or even regress. Sometimes you have to take the Star Trek mentality and think that if the green man gets shot, it is not for the good of one, but for the good of many. You do not want to sacrifice your program because one child will totally take control of all of your attention and energy.

If you are a behavior teacher you should know that the school, regardless of whether you believe it won't happen, will make you a so-called dumping ground for behavior students. You should have some safety nets in place so that you do not become the "dumping ground". The best thing a behavior teacher can do is to create a relationship with the school psychologist so they have a say in the referral process. Make sure that all the information about a child indicates an emotional disturbance, and that simple wording in the IEP is not slanted so you are pressured to take the child.

There are other options for the behavior student, other than the behavior program. They can have a tutor session off school grounds or they can be placed in a behavior treatment center. Preview the file carefully before agreeing. "You may even want to go to the child's classroom setting and get the opinions of the mainstream teachers or observe the child interacting in the class. This will allow you to see if the child should be in your program. You should not do anything to diminish the integrity of your program.

Tri Annual Testing

Every special education student needs to be tested both academically and behaviorally while they are attending special education programs. It is a special education teacher's duty to make sure assessment takes place. Some tests will be administered by psychologists, while others will be administered by doctors, or other professionals within the district. As the behavior teacher, you need to make sure the tests are conducted properly and that the compiler of all tests is available, to help determine if the child is determined to be a special education student. It is important that you as the teacher make every recommendation you can to either keep the child in special education or to dismiss them. Most of the time the child, especially a child in the behavior program, will not be dismissed from the program. It is only through resilient parents that this might happen.

Some parents have difficulty accepting that their child has a problem, especially if the problem is of a psychological nature. They may feel that their family's reputation or parenting skills are questionable. It is wise to have a psychologist on board to help you make decisions to present to the IEP team. Look at the dynamics of the child's home life, as well as outside influences the child might be involved with. As the behavior child gets older, drug and alcohol may become an issue. You should be aware of whether the parents support this deviant behavior, or if they knew nothing about it. You should also think about how the behavior child has grown over the past three years and what you, as the behavior teacher, can do to help the child grow successfully.

During the tri-annual testing, you may be asked to perform the Woodcock Johnson for the student. It is best to do this in your classroom or a location where they are comfortable. Taking them to a different room or taking them out of the school may make them feel anxious or they may feel emotions that will hinder them from doing their best on the test. You may have a student in your behavior classroom with a 120 IQ, but without the right testing environment you would never know about it. Test students only on days when they are comfortable and are not going through too many emotional problems.

Standardized District Testing

When it comes to state or national standardized district testing, the behavior child is put to many awkward positions. The test requires the student to sit and to answer questions they often times do not know the answer to, for long periods of time. This can be torturous for the behavior child. You as a behavior teacher have the option of taking all your children and have them tested in an insider classroom. You have to adhere to the state and national requirements for the testing and this may cause you to have to change or rumor on a little bit?

First thing you need to do is to clear all of your children's desks. In the behavior classroom, the desk of the behavior child is a place of solace where they can put their belongings and have a space to call their own. By clearing their desk were regular study occurs they aren't put at a risk of losing their security that they have within your room. Go over this process with your students so that they know that everything is going to be put back where it was after the testing is done. The students may show behaviors and you will have to deal with each behavior as the situation arises.

Some tests mandate that you clear all walls of anything that has words that could hold the child during the test. If you have any posters or word banks upon the wall don't take them down but simply cover them with some bulletin board backing paper. Just take some paper and tape over the words. In this way your room adheres to the rules of the test. You may also have to cover up bookshelves are other things that might produce words or sentences the child could use during the test.

Most behavior children have aversions to sound. Some behavior children have been known to not use a pencil because the sound of the pencil against the paper irritates them. These tests must be done with a number two pencil but you can supplement with a mechanical pencil. If a child has a severe sensitivity to sound you may put a headphone on the child so that he or she will not be aggravated by the sound.

Most tests mandate that the child be given the same learning tools they have in the classroom. This could include a dictionary or thesaurus, but it is wise to check with your test administrator to see if the glossary is appropriate for the test that your state uses? Also check to see if protractors, compasses in capital letters are needed. In some cases the test administrators will have a computer-based math test in which these tools are already incorporated?

During the test you need to take a long break for the children to unwind. Most of the students will have extended time as modified on their IEP. You should be able to, if you are on a writing section of the test, let the children write for 15 to 20 minutes and then let them have a break. You might want to just walk around the school routes to let the children stretch their legs and clear their minds. This may be frowned upon by administration or other teachers but your children are special and need that extra time to get their mind clear.

Another strategy during test taking is to allow the students to listen to music on their headphones while they are taking the test. Some of these children cannot have any outside distractions and can work amazingly with their own music in the background. Again this may be frowned upon by administration, but you have to have some special allotments with these kids.

During the math portion of these standardized tests, most of the children will freeze. Most children hate math and for them to have to do math problems in which they have no clue, is torturous to their young minds. But the minute they get into the test there will be questions that they will not be able to answer. Do not let the students know there are questions that even you as a teacher do not know. This test is to measure what they know and they cannot pass or fail.

Some teachers stress to their students that if they fail these standardized tests, they may be held back a grade. Do not make this kind of threat to the behavior student. Let them do their best without a threat and be supportive while they are taking the test. You might want to offer rewards to a student that has made significant gains from the last round of tests. This will allow you to be able to give the child something to work for. You may also want to give small rewards during the test taking time. If a child finishes early before the others, have a space set aside for them so they can quietly do that can be they like to do. Those that finish early should stay away from the other testers because most behavior children will lose control and work something out loud or will cause a commotion if not on task?

Modified Assessments

When you are developing AE IEP for a behavior student, you should keep in mind that you need to modify the IEP so that the child will receive modifications and accommodations from their classroom assessments. Test taking is a hard thing for a behavior child and for them to lose academic standing because they do not do well in testing should not be a consideration. The child should be able to restrain their knowledge of the concept or skill in ways that are outside the norm in the regular classroom.

One of the modifications a teacher can help implement into the IEP is extended time. If the child feels that they are on a time limit, they may make more mistakes or even have a breakdown during the test. The test anxiety is an infliction that many people experience, but to the behavior child, the emotions of test anxiety will be if applied and they may even have a melt down during the assessment?

Another modification could be that the child is assessed differently than other children. If the child can express their knowledge of the concept verbally instead of writing it down, this could be a good way for the teacher to know that the child understands the concept. Most behavior children hate to write and combine with writing in the assessment, the results could be disastrous. If the child starts squirming in their seat or show signs of test anxiety, just take the test and see if they can answer the questions after a break.

The assessment can be altered in a way that the child understands .Younger behavior children have a hard time with out-of-the-box thinking. If the question asked of them is to compare and contrast, then the teacher or paraprofessional should rephrase the question in a way that the child can understand. Instead of comparing contrast, a teacher could ask the student to tell them what is difference between the two items and what is the same. Once they learn the terms "compare" and "contrast" the transition will be easier, but you should be able to paraphrase a question in a way they will understand so that they will have some success in the assessment.

During preparations for an assessment, modifications are again important. The teacher or paraprofessional can use flashcards, memory games, or a hundred different other methods that are non-traditional. The behavior child will adjust to one method or another, and once you find out what works for preparing for the assessment, that is the choice you should use for every assessment until the child turns against it. Processing with a child about the assessment can be tricky. The most important thing for the teacher is to remember that the child should be able to show what they have learned beyond the paper and pencil test. When the child shows success in assessment, and the child's self-esteem and self-worth will expand and the assessments will not be as stressful the next time.

Working with the Mainstream Teacher

One of the main problems that a behavior teacher will find is working with a mainstream teacher. Many mainstream teachers do not understand behavior children, nor do they understand what disabilities the children have. You, as a behavior teacher, need to consult with the mainstream teacher before the child comes into their class. It is a sad occurrence, but some teachers refuse to recognize the emotional disability and think of that student is just a bad person. Most teachers do not want behavior children in their classroom and so you become the alternative.

Once you hurtled the barrier of introducing the child into the classroom, you and the teacher need to sit down and go over what the child's issues are. Give as much information about the child as you can to the teacher and let them ask questions and help you create strategies. You might want to make recommendations about assignments, modifications, and accommodations. You or the paraprofessional will be with the child during the entire time they are in the mainstream classroom. This is, of course, if the student has reached a level where they can go unsupervised into the classroom.

Let the mainstream teacher know your expectations of behavior. Though you do not want to have expectations higher than the other kids in the class, you should at least share the basics of your program. Do not expect the mainstream teacher to work your program for you. If the teacher has problems with the child they should call you immediately so that you can remove the child from the room. Let them have your cell phone number and though cell phones are not permitted in schools in most states, you as a behavior teacher need to be on call at all times to assist with your student's behaviors.

The mainstream teachers should have a right to ask the child to leave the room and even though you may think the child's behavior is not that disturbing the other students. You should respect the teacher's wishes. If this child becomes out-of-control they shall lose the right remain in that level of their program. Once the child loses their mainstream privileges they are eager to gain them back. If the teacher is still resistant to the child being in their class, ask if there is a position available in another classroom with another teacher. Some teachers just cannot work with behavior children and you will have to accept it. It may seem these teachers are not doing their job but they have to look out for their class, which cannot be put in jeopardy for one child.

Drugs and Alcohol with the Behavior Student

Some of your students will come from families where drugs are an issue. They grew up around and drugs and alcohol and may have parents incarcerated because of illegal substances. If you teach older behavior students, you need to be aware of the signs of drug and alcohol abuse. If you can stop the abuse before it gets out of control you may save the child a life of sadness and incarceration.

With the behavior child and with the emotionally disabled, it is hard to judge the mood of your students. Sometimes they are happy and easy-going while other times are depressed and sad. These are the signs of drug dependency, but it could also be the sign of an emotional disorder. The disorder could give the same symptoms of someone coming down from a high or hung over the following morning.

This means you really have to watch your children and know their habits. If you are teaching the older high school age students, drug and alcohol is a part of their culture. They will experiment just like any other non-special education child. Watch for redness in the eyes and a tendency to be tired in the mornings.

Though this is some signs of prescribed medications and also can be a sign that your child has been abusing either alcohol or drugs.

If you do suspect the student of being intoxicated, do not confront them by yourself. Alert a member of the administration to the current situation and have them there for support. If you become known as the person who got the child into trouble with authorities, the trust that you built during the school year is lost and you will have a hard time gaining the trust back again. The administration's job is to deal with drug issues and the best thing for you to do, as the behavior teacher, is to let them do it.

Make sure you have hard evidence that the child is using alcohol or drugs before you go to the administration. The child may be on the low or high cycle of their bipolar disorder or they may simply have a medication change. Talk to the parents and see what they think about the situation and if they have any suspicions before you move forward. Punishing the child is not the way to stop them from abusing drugs and alcohol. Try to get them into a rehab or to a counselor's office to confront the problem.

If your student tells you their parents have drug or alcohol issues you need to contact the counselor's office immediately. They are the counselor to conduct a DFS and they can make a home visit to see if the child is reporting accurately. Unfortunately alcohol abuse is not illegal but the actions caused by alcohol could put the child in harm.

Medications and the Behavior Child

Many of the students in your classroom will be on medications. This is to help them get through the day and to also help build and treat various disorders whether they are mental or physical. You should not have any dealings with the medications. The medications should be given to the nurse and distributed at the time that it is prescribed. You should be responsible for getting the child down to the nurse at the proper time to the child may get their medications.

An ADHD child or any child that has a hyper active disorder may go off the deep end if they do not have their medications. You will see a serious fluctuation of moods or you may see the child be so hyperactive they cannot even sit in their seat. Not only will this behavior affect the child's education but their behavior also affects the education of others.

Now Go Out There and Teach

As I stated in the first chapter, this is not an official guideline of research-based documentation, as a derivative. These are my personal experiences and I want to share them, not only with the behavior teacher, but also with a mainstream teacher who will pick up a copy of this book and be able to understand the emotionally disabled or the behavior contact student a little better.

Remember when you teach in the behavior classroom you are on the defensive at every moment. You are not only on the defensive from your students and their behaviors, but also from the administration and the mainstream teacher population at your school. Even some parents may hold something against you because they think that the kids in a behavior classroom are rotten kids. On the contrary, they are full of love and happiness and they can foster into a productive citizen, just like any other normal child.

Remember that you are a breed of your own as a behavior teacher. Not many people understand what you do and some people may even criticize your methods. If something does not work try something else. Ask for guidance from other special education teachers. Even though you may not have experience in the behavior field, they will surely be the behavior expert for your school site. You will be asked to come to more meetings than you can count because they want your advice on the behavior of the child.

You will be even asked to come to non-special education meetings to advise others with your opinion on how they should treat a certain child. Get used to it. After only a few weeks of teaching in a behavior classroom, you will be considered an expert.

Remember that you are there for your children and your students. Your room has become a safe haven where the administration, other teachers, and other students cannot touch the children. The students need to know that this safe place will be there with them until they are ready to leave your program. In return for providing a safe place, you will find an unbridled love the no mainstream teacher will ever feel. You will develop relationships with your children that have bonds far beyond the normal relationships between student and teacher.

2935386

Made in the USA